D1283645

PAINT EFFECTS
for walls and surfaces

PAINT EFFECTS
for walls and surfaces

Over 25 inspirational ways to transform your home with paint, including sponging, colourwashing, stippling, stencilling and stamping, with over 300 colour photographs

sacha cohen and maggie philo

southwater

This edition is published by Southwater

Southwater is an imprint of Anness Publishing Ltd
Hermes House, 88–89 Blackfriars Road, London SE1 8HA
tel. 020 7401 2077; fax 020 7633 9499
www.southwaterbooks.com; info@anness.com

© Anness Publishing Ltd 2005

UK agent: The Manning Partnership Ltd, 6 The Old Dairy,
Melcombe Road, Bath BA2 3LR; tel. 01225 478444;
fax 01225 478440; sales@manning-partnership.co.uk

UK distributor: Grantham Book Services Ltd, Isaac Newton Way,
Alma Park Industrial Estate, Grantham, Lincs NG31 9SD;
tel. 01476 541080; fax 01476 541061; orders@gbs.tbs-ltd.co.uk

North American agent/distributor: National Book Network,
4501 Forbes Boulevard, Suite 200, Lanham, MD 20706;
tel. 301 459 3366; fax 301 429 5746; www.nbnbooks.com

Australian agent/distributor: Pan Macmillan Australia,
Level 18, St Martins Tower,
31 Market St,
Sydney, NSW 2000;
tel. 1300 135 113; fax 1300 135 103;
customer.service@macmillan.com.au

New Zealand agent/distributor: David Bateman Ltd,
30 Tarndale Grove, Off Bush Road,
Albany, Auckland;
tel. (09) 415 7664; fax (09) 415 8892

A CIP catalogue record for this book is available from the British Library.

Publisher: Joanna Lorenz
Editorial Director: Judith Simons
Project Editor: Felicity Forster
Copy Editor: Judy Cox
Photographers: Lizzie Orme and Adrian Taylor

Project Contributors: Petra Boase, Sacha Cohen, Lucinda
Ganderton, Elaine Green, Emma Hardy and Liz Wagstaff
Stylists: Katie Gibbs and Judy Williams
Designer: Bill Mason
Production Controller: Claire Rae

Previously published as part of a larger volume, *Paint Effects Projects*

1 3 5 7 9 10 8 6 4 2

CONTENTS

INTRODUCTION

Home decorating is not simply a matter of painting your walls with white emulsion (latex); there is a wealth of different paints in amazing colours, and many original, easy ways to apply them. With just a little imagination and a lot of fun, you can create originality and colour throughout your home. This book brings together the easiest and most adaptable of decorative paint techniques, with fabulous ideas for applying them to the surfaces of your home. The projects range from the simple to the more complicated, so there is something for every level of expertise and ability. Each project is explained fully with clear step-by-step instructions and photographs. You will find many ideas for overhauling a whole room – why not create instant limewashed walls or stunning imitation Moorish tiles? Alternatively, you can use stencils and

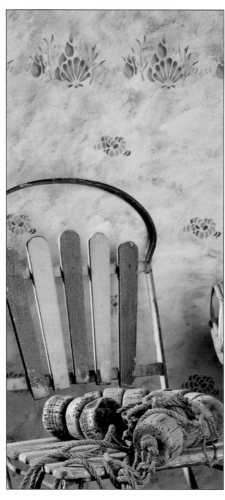

stamps to add distinctive patterns of folk-art tulips, celestial cherubs or animal friezes to a wall. The book also contains invaluable advice about materials, equipment and techniques – which brushes, sponges, rollers and paints to choose, and how to mix paints to create fantastic new palettes of colour. There are step-by-step instructions that explain how to design and cut your own stencils and stamps as well as how to master a wide range of paint effects. Simple effects include sponging, colourwashing, combing and dragging, while more complicated effects include block stencilling, two-colour stippling, flicking, making drop-shadows and varnishing. A templates section at the back of the book will allow you to create professional-looking designs. Armed with this compendium of decorative projects, you will never be short of inspiration.

MATERIALS,
EQUIPMENT AND
TECHNIQUES

The most important requirement for successful results in applying paint effects is the proper use of the correct materials and equipment. With many of the techniques you can achieve stunning decoration with ordinary household paintbrushes, rollers, sponges and artist's brushes, but specialist equipment is needed for some effects. These items are available in decorators' suppliers and craft shops, where you can also ask for advice on their use. Choose good-quality materials. Make sure that you have the type of paint suitable for the specific technique you are planning. Practise the painting, stencilling and stamping techniques in this section before beginning any of the projects.

ABOVE: Every home decorator needs a good selection of paintbrushes, measuring equipment, sponges and rollers.

LEFT: Once mastered, the technique of stencilling can be used for elaborate designs, such as this heraldic dining room.

PAINTING MATERIALS

Acrylic or emulsion (latex) paint and acrylic scumble glaze are the main painting materials that you will need to put a wide variety of paint techniques into practice.

Acrylic primer is a quick-drying water-based primer. It is used to prime new wood.

Acrylic scumble is a slow-drying, water-based medium with a milky, gel-like appearance, which dries clear. It adds texture and translucency to the paint, and the marks you make with brushes, sponges and other tools are held in the glaze.

Acrylic varnish is available in a satin or matt (flat) finish. It is used to seal paint effects to give a more durable and protective finish to the surface. Acrylic floor varnish is extremely hardwearing and should be used on floors.

Artist's acrylic paint can be found in art and craft shops and comes in a wide range of colours. It gives various paint effects a subtle translucent quality.

Crackle glaze is brushed on to a surface, causing the paint laid over it to crack in random patterns to create an aged appearance.

Emulsion paint is opaque and comes in a choice of matt (flat) or satin finish. Satin finish is best for the base colour and matt for paint effects. Use sample pots of paint if you need only a small amount.

Methylated spirits (methyl alcohol) is a solvent that will dissolve emulsion (latex) paint and can therefore be used to distress paint. It is also used as a solvent, thinner and brush cleaner for shellac.

Pure powder pigment can be used to colour paint and can be mixed with acrylic scumble, clear wax or emulsion (latex) paint. It is also used for vinegar graining.

Shellac is a type of varnish, which is available in clear and brown shades. French polish and button polish are in fact shellac and may be easier to find. Shellac can be used to seal wood, metal leaf and paint.

Wax is available in neutral and in brown. It will seal and colour paint. Neutral wax can be mixed with powder pigment.

RIGHT: 1 powder pigments, 2 emulsion (latex) paints, 3 acrylic primer, 4 artist's acrylic paint, 5 acrylic scumble, 6 crackle glaze, 7 neutral wax, 8 brown wax, 9 methylated spirits (methyl alcohol), 10 brown shellac, 11 clear shellac.

STENCILLING MATERIALS

Avariety of materials can be used for stencilling, from specialist stencilling paints and sticks to acrylics and emulsion (latex). Each has its own properties and will create different effects.

Acrylic stencil paints

These are quick-drying paints, reducing the chance of the paint running and seeping behind the stencil. Acrylic stencil paints are available in a wide range of colours and can be mixed to create more subtle shades.

Acrylic varnish

This is useful for sealing and protecting finished projects.

Emulsion paints

Ordinary household emulsion (latex) can also be used for stencilling. It is best to avoid the cheaper varieties as these contain a lot of water and will seep through the stencil.

Fabric paints

These are used in the same way as acrylic stencil paints, and come in an equally wide range of colours, which can be mixed to create your own shades. Fixed with an iron according to the manufacturer's instructions, they will withstand washing and everyday use. As with ordinary acrylic stencil paints do not overload the brush with colour, as it will seep into the fabric. Always back the fabric you are stencilling with scrap paper or newspaper to prevent the paints from marking the work surface.

Gold leaf and gold size

These can be used to spectacular effect. The actual design is stencilled with gold size. The size is then left to become tacky and the gold leaf rubbed over the design.

Metallic creams

These are available in many different metallic finishes, from gold through to bronze and copper and silver. Metallic creams can be applied as highlights on a painted base, or used for the entire design. They can be applied with cloths or your fingertip.

Oil-based stencil sticks and creams

The sticks can be used in the same way as a wax crayon, while the creams can be applied with a brush, cloth or your fingertip. With any method, there is no danger of overloading the colour, and they won't run. The disadvantage is their long drying time (can be overnight in some cases); also, the colours can become muddy when mixed. Sticks and creams are also available for use on fabrics.

RIGHT: 1 acrylic stencil paints, 2 oil-based cream and metallic creams, 3 fabric paints, 4 oil-based stencil sticks, 5 emulsion (latex) paints, 6 gold leaf, 7 acrylic varnish, 8 gold size.

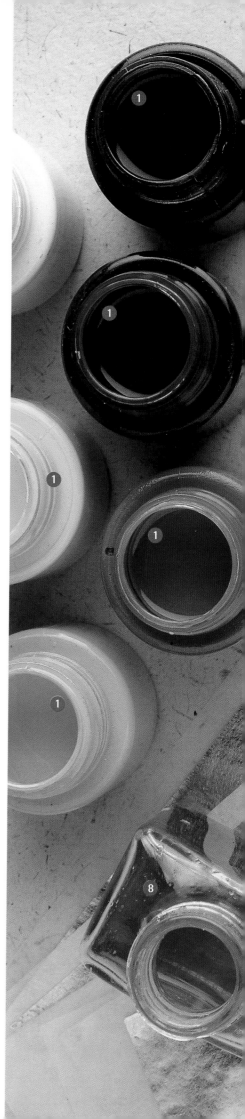

STAMPING MATERIALS

Stamps can be constructed from a variety of materials, and a whole range of exciting and stylish effects can be achieved by combining different paints and inks with your chosen stamps.

Dutch metal leaf and gold size
Metal leaf is a cheap, easy-to-use alternative to real gold leaf. Use a sponge stamp to apply gold size in a repeating pattern. When the size is tacky, apply the gold leaf.

Inks
Water-based inks are too runny to use on their own but can be added to wallpaper paste or varnish to make a mixture thick enough to adhere to the stamp. Use them for paper or card (stock), but not for walls. If you are using rubber stamps, inkpads are commercially available in a range of colours.

Interior filler
Add filler, in its dry powdered state, to emulsion (latex) paint to give it body without diluting the colour.

Paint
Water-based paints such as emulsion and artist's acrylics dry quickly to a permanent finish. Use emulsion paint straight from the can or dilute it with wallpaper paste or varnish. For wall treatments, emulsion paint can be thinned with water and sponged or brushed over the wall as a colourwash.

Pre-cut stamps
Rubber stamps are widely available in thousands of designs. Finely detailed motifs are best suited to small-scale projects, while bolder shapes are best for walls and also furniture.

Sponge or foam
Different types of sponge are characterized by their density. High-density sponge is best for detailed shapes and will give a smooth, sharp print. Medium-density sponge or low-density sponge will absorb more paint and give a more textured result.

Varnish
Use water-based acrylic varnish (sold as quick-drying) for stamping projects. It can be mixed with emulsion paint or ink to thicken the texture and create a range of different sheens. The varnish will also protect and preserve the design of your stamp.

Wallpaper paste
This allows you to thin emulsion paint without making it too runny to adhere to the stamp. Mix up the paste with the required amount of water first, then add the emulsion.

RIGHT: 1 Dutch metal leaf and gold size, 2 coloured inks, 3 low-density sponge, 4 pre-cut stamp, 5 high-density sponge, 6 medium-density sponges, 7 interior filler, 8 emulsion (latex) paint, 9 varnish, 10 wallpaper paste.

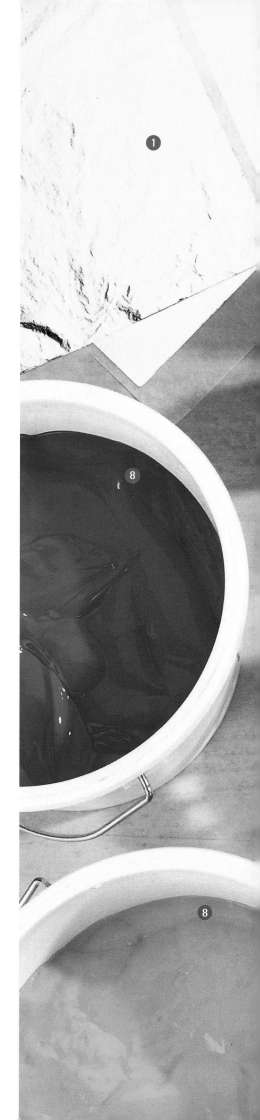

PAINTING EQUIPMENT

Different paint effects require different tools. Most of the tools illustrated are cheap and they are easily found in do-it-yourself or decorating suppliers.

Abrasives include abrasive paper and wire (steel) wool, which come in many grades. They are used for distressing paint.

Artist's paintbrushes are needed to paint fine detail.

Decorator's paintbrushes are used to apply emulsion (latex) paint, washes and glazes. They come in a wide range of sizes.

Flat varnish brushes can be used for painting and varnishing. They are often the choice of the experts.

Masking tape comes in many types. Easy-mask and low-tack tapes are less likely to pull off paintwork, and flexible tape is good for going around curves. Fine line tape is useful for creating a narrow negative line.

Measuring equipment such as a ruler, spirit level, set square (T square) and plumbline are needed to mark out designs.

Mutton cloth is very absorbent and can be used for paint effects. Cotton cloths are also used for ragging and polishing.

Natural sponges are used for sponging. They are valued for their textural quality. Synthetic sponges can be used for colourwashing.

Paint containers such as paint kettles, trays and pots are used to mix and store paint.

Paint rollers, small and large, are used to provide an even-textured base colour without brushmarks. They are also used to create textured paint effects.

Rubber combs and heart grainers are used to create textured patterns in paint glazes. Heart grainers (rockers) create an effect of the heart grain of wood.

Softening brushes are used for blending colours together.

Stencil brushes are for stippling paint on to smaller surfaces.

Stippling brushes are usually rectangular, and are used to even out the texture of glaze and to avoid brushmarks.

RIGHT: *1 paint containers, 2 spirit level, 3 plumbline, 4 kitchen paper, 5 artist's brushes, 6 decorator's brushes, 7 flat varnish brushes, 8 hog softening brush, 9 stencil brush, 10 paint rollers, 11 gloves, 12 stippling brush, 13 masking tapes, 14 measuring equipment, 15 craft knife and pencil, 16 heart grainer (rocker), 17 combs, 18 natural and synthetic sponges, 19 mutton cloth (stockinet), 20 rag, 21 wire (steel) wool and abrasive paper.*

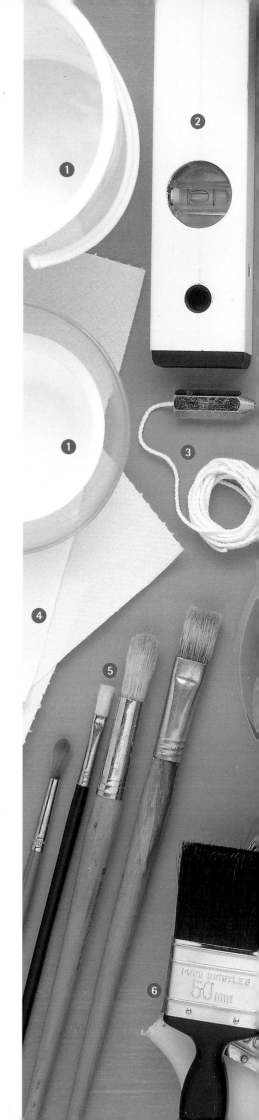

STENCILLING EQUIPMENT

Stencilling does not require a great deal of specialist equipment; many of the items used are commonly found in most households. Some additional items, however, will make the job easier.

Brushes
It is worth investing in a set of good stencil brushes. The ends of the brushes should be flat and the bristles firm, to allow you to control the application of paint. A medium-sized brush (3cm/1^{1}/$_{2}$in diameter) is a useful, all-purpose size, but you may want to buy one size smaller and one size larger as well. You will need a selection of household paintbrushes for applying large areas of background colour, and small artist's paintbrushes for adding fine details.

Craft knife
Use for cutting out stencils from card (stock).

Self-healing cutting mat
This provides a firm surface to cut into and will help prevent the craft knife from slipping. Mats come in a range of sizes and are commonly printed with a grid and imperial or metric measures for accurate and quick cutting.

Masking tape
As the stencil may need to be repositioned it is advisable to hold it in place with masking tape, which can be removed fairly easily.

Paint-mixing container
This may be necessary for mixing paints and colourwashes.

Pencils
Keep a selection of both soft and hard pencils to transfer the stencil design on to card (stock). Use an ordinary pencil to mark the positions of the stencils before applying.

Stencil card
The material used to make the stencil is a matter of personal preference. Special stencil card (stock) is available waxed, which means that it will last longer, but ordinary card or heavy paper can also be used. It is worth purchasing a sheet of clear acetate if you wish to keep your stencil design. This means that you will be able to reuse the design for future projects.

Tape measure and straight-edges
Many stencilling projects require accurate positioning. Measuring and planning the design and layout of your stencils before you begin will aid the result.

Tracing paper
Use this to transfer your stencil design on to stencil card (stock).

RIGHT: 1 sraight-edges, 2 tape measure, 3 stencil brushes, 4 household paintbrush, 5 self-healing cutting mat, 6 stencil card (stock), 7 tracing paper, 8 soft pencil, 9 craft knife, 10 paint-mixing container, 11 masking tape.

STAMPING EQUIPMENT

Stamping is a very simple craft and does not require a great deal of specialist equipment. Most of the items illustrated here will already be found in an ordinary household.

Craft knife and self-healing cutting mat

A sharp-bladed craft knife is essential for cutting your own stamps out of sponge. Use a self-healing cutting mat to protect your work surface, and always direct the blade away from your fingers.

Linoleum blocks

These are available from art and craft shops and can be cut to make stamps which recreate the look of a wood block. You'll need special linoleum-cutting tools, which are also easily available, to scoop out the areas around the design. Always hold the linoleum with your spare hand behind your cutting hand for safety.

Masking tape

Use for masking off areas of walls and furniture.

Natural sponge

Use for applying colourwashes to walls and other larger surfaces before stamping.

Paintbrushes

A range of decorator's brushes is needed for painting furniture and walls before stamping. Use a broad brush to apply colourwashes to walls. Stiff brushes can be used to stipple paint on to stamps for textured effects, while finer brushes are used to pick out details or to apply paint to the stamp.

Pencils, pens and crayons

Use a soft pencil to trace templates for stamps, and for making easily removable guidelines on walls. Draw motifs freehand using a felt-tipped pen on medium- and low-density sponge. Use a white crayon on black upholstery foam.

Rags

Keep a stock of clean rags and cloths for cleaning stamps and preparing surfaces.

Ruler and tape measure

Use these to plan your design.

Scissors

Use sharp scissors to cut out medium- and low-density sponge shapes and also for cutting out templates.

Sponge rollers

Small paint rollers can be used to load your stamps. You will need several if you are stamping in different colours.

RIGHT: 1 scissors, 2 craft knife, 3 masking tape, 4 paint rollers, 5 ruler, 6 tape measure, 7 pencils, 8 self-healing cutting mat, 9 rag, 10 natural sponge, 11 paintbrushes.

PAINTING TECHNIQUES

A number of the projects in this book are based on a few simple techniques that can either be used on their own or combined to produce an infinite variety of paint effects. The techniques shown here all use ultramarine blue emulsion (latex) paint. This has been mixed with acrylic scumble glaze and/or water, as appropriate, to achieve the desired effect. Two coats of satin finish white emulsion paint were rollered on as a base. This provides an even-textured, non-absorbent finish, which is ideal to work on as it allows glazes to dry more slowly and evenly than emulsion paint. It also means that if you make any mistakes they are easily wiped off. All these techniques, except the crackle glaze, can be done with artist's acrylic paint mixed with scumble, in which case the effects will look more translucent.

Sponging

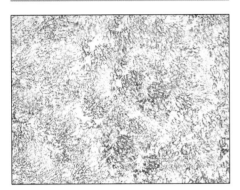

Dilute a little paint with a little water in a paint tray or on a saucer. Dip a damp natural sponge into the paint and wipe off the excess on kitchen paper. Dab the sponge evenly on to the prepared surface in different directions.

Sponging and dispersion

Follow the technique as for sponging, then rinse the sponge in clean water and dab it over the sponged paint before it dries to soften the effect.

Combing

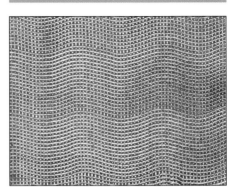

Mix the paint with acrylic scumble and brush on with cross-hatched brushstrokes. Run a metal or rubber graining comb through the wet glaze to make a pattern. This pattern was done with straight vertical strokes followed by wavy horizontal ones.

Colourwashing

Dilute the paint with water and brush on randomly with cross-hatched brushstrokes, using a large decorator's brush. Alternatively, a damp sponge will give a similar effect.

Rubbing in colourwash

Dilute the paint with water and brush on. Use a clean cotton rag to disperse the paint. Alternatively, apply it directly with the rag and rub in.

Frottage

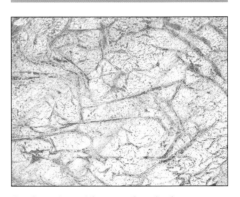

Apply paint with cross-hatched brushstrokes, then press a piece of tissue paper over the wet surface and peel it off. The paint can be diluted with water or scumble.

Dabbing with a mutton cloth

Brush on paint mixed with scumble, using cross-hatched brushstrokes. Dab a mutton cloth (stockinet) over the wet glaze to even out the texture and eliminate the brushstrokes.

Ragging

Mix paint with scumble and brush on, using cross-hatched brushstrokes. Scrunch up a piece of cotton rag and dab this on the wet paint in all directions, twisting your hand for a random look. When the rag becomes too paint-soaked, use a new one.

Rag rolling without brushmarks

Brush on paint mixed with scumble and dab with a mutton cloth (stockinet) to eliminate brushmarks. Scrunch a cotton rag into a sausage shape and roll over the surface, changing direction as you go. Use a new piece of rag when it becomes too wet.

Stippling

Brush on paint mixed with acrylic scumble, using cross-hatched brushstrokes. Pounce a stippling brush over the wet glaze, working from the bottom upwards to eliminate brushmarks and provide an even-textured surface. Keep the brush as dry as possible by regularly wiping the bristles with kitchen paper.

Dragging

Mix paint with scumble glaze and brush on with cross-hatched brushstrokes. Drag a flat decorator's brush through the wet glaze, keeping a steady hand. The soft effect shown here is achieved by going over the wet glaze a second time to break up the vertical lines.

Crackle glaze

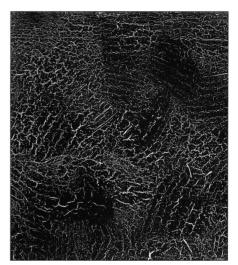

Brush on a coat of water-based crackle glaze and leave to dry according to the manufacturer's instructions. Using a well-laden brush, apply paint carefully on top so that you lay, rather than brush, it over the surface. Work quickly and do not overbrush an area already painted. If you have missed an area, touch it in when the paint has dried. Seal with acrylic varnish.

MIXING PAINTS AND GLAZES

There are no precise recipes for mixing glazes and washes. Generally, the proportion of emulsion (latex) paint to scumble is 1 part paint to 6 parts scumble. This will give soft, semi-translucent colour that is suitable for effects such as ragging, dragging and combing where you want the coloured glaze to hold the marks you have made. You can reduce the amount of scumble if you want a more opaque coverage. However the paint will dry more quickly so it may be harder to maintain a wet edge for an even result. When you are mixing scumble with artist's acrylic paint, the amount of paint you should use depends on the depth of colour you need. Acrylic paint mixed with scumble gives a more translucent colour. It is used in exactly the same way as the emulsion glazes and washes.

If you do not need the texture provided by the scumble (for example, when colourwashing) but you want to dilute the colour, use water. This is cheaper but it dries more quickly, which may be a disadvantage. If you want to slow down the drying time, add a 50/50 mix of water and scumble to the paint. Emulsion paint can be diluted with any amount of water, and several thin washes of colour will give a more even cover than one thick wash.

Try to mix up enough colour to complete the area you are to decorate. Washes and glazes stretch a long way, but if in doubt, mix up more than you think you might need. If you want to repeat the effect, measure the quantities you use. Before you start, painting samples on to scrap wood will give you the truest effect.

Ragging with acrylic paint and scumble.

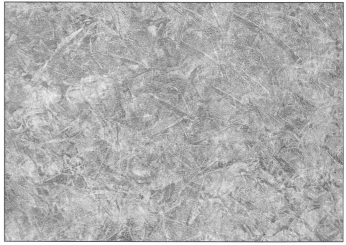

Ragging with emulsion (latex) paint and scumble.

Colourwashing with one wash of equal parts emulsion (latex) paint and water.

Colourwashing with four thin washes of 1 part paint to 8 parts water to achieve the same colour saturation.

WORKING WITH COLOUR

Paint effects can vary widely according to your choice of colour and the way in which you use it. Whether you put a light colour over a dark base or a dark colour over a light one is a matter of choice, although a translucent pale colour would not really be visible over a dark base. A bright base colour can give added depth and a subtle glow beneath a dark top coat, while using the colours the other way round will tone down a bright colour. Tone-on-tone colour combinations are good for a subtle effect and are always a safe bet, but experiment with contrasting colours for exciting results.

Some of the projects featured in this book use layers of several different colours. Greater depth and texture are achieved when you build up colours in this way, but a simple technique with one colour can be just as effective. It depends on the look you want and the furnishings in the room.

If you want to tone down a paint effect, you can lighten it by brushing over a wash of very diluted white or off-white emulsion (latex) paint. You can also tone down a colour by darkening it. A wash of raw umber paint works well over most colours and has a much warmer feel than black.

Adding white to lighten bright blue colourwashing.

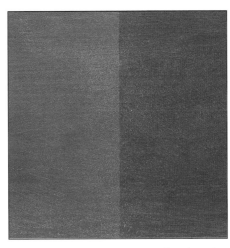

Adding raw umber to darken bright red colourwashing.

Sponging – light yellow over deep yellow (left), deep yellow over light yellow (right).

Dabbing with a mutton cloth (stockinet) – dull green over emerald green (left), emerald green over dull green (right).

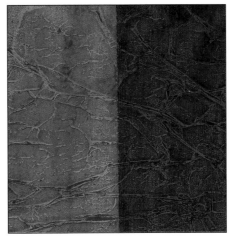

Frottage – tone-on-tone, deep blue over light blue (left), two tones of contrasting colours, bright blue over orange (right).

Colourwashing (left) in orange, red and crimson, finishing with the darkest colour on the top surface. Layers of sponging (right) in three shades of blue-green, finishing with the lightest colour on the top surface.

MIXING COLOURS

Emulsion (latex) paint is available in a huge range of ready-mixed colours. If you use acrylic paint or pure powder pigment you will need to mix your own colours.

Most colours can be mixed from yellow, cyan blue, magenta, black and white, but a basic palette of 14 colours plus black and white will allow you to mix an enormous range of colours. The suggested palette consists of yellow ochre, cadmium yellow, raw sienna, burnt sienna, red ochre, cadmium red, alizarin crimson, ultramarine blue, Prussian blue, cerulean blue, viridian green, oxide of chromium, raw umber and burnt umber. These basic colours are beautiful alone, and many other colours can be made by mixing them.

Some colour combinations are unexpected, and there are no hard-and-fast rules about which colours should or should not be mixed. If you experiment, you will soon develop confidence and a good eye for mixing colour.

Yellows and browns (right)

1 *Cadmium yellow and white*

2 *Cadmium yellow*

3 *Cadmium yellow and*
  viridian green

4 *Yellow ochre and white*

5 *Yellow ochre*

6 *Raw sienna*

7 *Burnt sienna*

8 *Burnt umber*

9 *Raw umber*

Reds

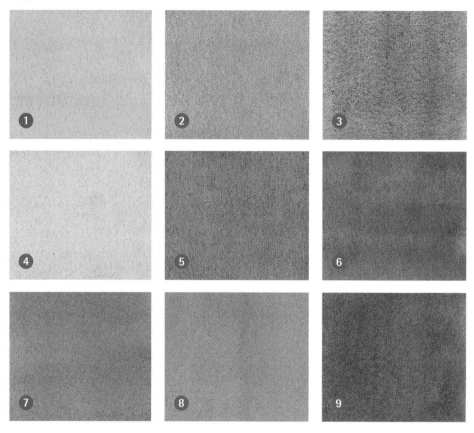

Yellows and browns

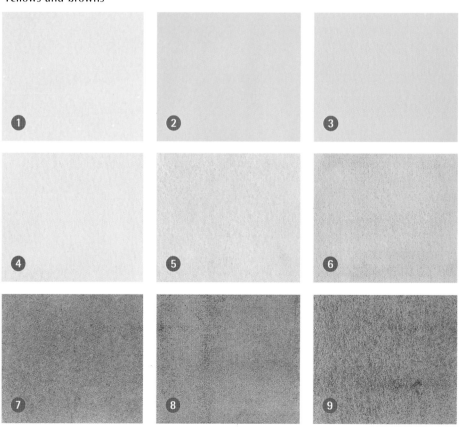

Reds (opposite)

1 *Alizarin crimson, cadmium yellow and white*
2 *Cadmium red and cadmium yellow*
3 *Red ochre*
4 *Red ochre and white*
5 *Cadmium red and burnt umber*
6 *Cadmium red*
7 *Cadmium red and black*
8 *Alizarin crimson*
9 *Alizarin crimson and oxide of chromium*

Blues (top right)

1 *Cerulean blue, raw umber and white*
2 *Prussian blue, black and white*
3 *Prussian blue*
4 *Cerulean blue*
5 *Ultramarine blue and white*
6 *Ultramarine blue*
7 *Alizarin crimson, ultramarine blue and white*
8 *Alizarin crimson and ultramarine blue*
9 *Ultramarine blue and raw umber*

Greens (right)

1 *Prussian blue and yellow ochre*
2 *Prussian blue and cadmium yellow*
3 *Prussian blue, cadmium yellow and white*
4 *Ultramarine and yellow ochre*
5 *Oxide of chromium*
6 *Viridian green and cadmium yellow*
7 *Viridian green*
8 *Viridian green, raw umber and white*
9 *Prussian blue, yellow ochre and white*

Blues

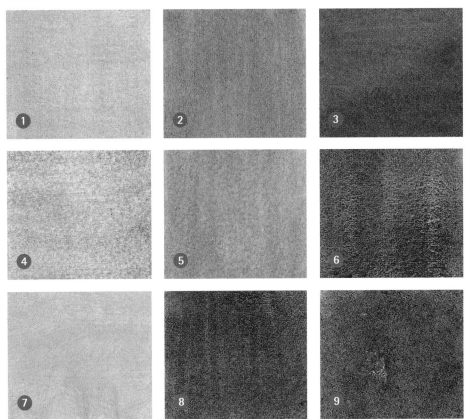

Greens

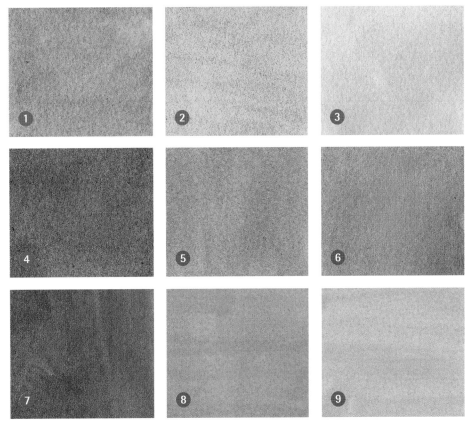

27

STENCILLING TECHNIQUES

Stencilling is not difficult to master, but it is worth practising on a small area to get used to handling the stencil brush and to become accustomed to the properties of the various paints you use. The techniques illustrated below show you how to make your own stencils and different ways in which to use them.

TRANSFERRING TEMPLATES

1 To transfer a template on to a piece of stencil card (stock), place a piece of tracing paper over the design, and draw over it with a hard pencil.

2 Turn over the tracing paper, and on the back of the design rub over the lines you have drawn, this time using a soft pencil.

3 Turn the design back to the right side and place on a sheet of stencil card. Draw over the original lines with a hard pencil.

CUTTING STENCILS

1 Place the tracing paper design on to a self-healing cutting mat or piece of thick card (stock) and secure in place with masking tape. Use a craft knife for cutting along the pencil lines.

2 It is safer to move the cutting board towards you and the craft knife when you are working round awkward shapes. Continue to cut out the design, moving the board as necessary.

STENCILLING EFFECTS

Block stencilling in a single solid colour

Use for filling in large areas in a single solid colour. As in all stencilling, remember not to apply the paint too heavily – less is more. Always blot out the paint on to a piece of blotting card (stock) before you begin.

Block stencilling with second colour stippled

When applying two colours, always apply the lighter shade first, then the darker. Do not cover the entire surface with the first colour; leave a gap for the second shade, then blend later. Use a separate, clean brush for each colour.

Block stencilling in two colours

When you apply the first colour, do not fully block out the petals; instead, outline them with the first colour and leave the centres bare. Use the second colour to fill. Take care not to apply the paint too heavily.

Rotating with blocked leaves

Using a very dry brush with a tiny amount of paint, rotate the bristles in a circular motion. This rotating action leaves enough paint on the surface for a lighter, softer look than a block application. Use the same effect in a darker colour on the inside of the petals.

Rotating and soft shading

Using a very dry brush with a tiny amount of paint, place your brush on one side of the stencil and rotate the brush in small circles. Repeat this action, using a slightly darker colour on the edges of the stencil, to create the effect of soft shading.

Rotating and shading in two colours

This is a similar effect to rotating and shading, but is more directional. Using a very dry brush with a tiny amount of paint, place your brush in the centre of the flower and rotate the bristles slightly outwards. Repeat this action, using a slightly darker colour.

Brushing up and down

Using slightly more paint on your brush than you would for rotating, brush up and down only, taking care to keep the lines vertical.

Dry brushing with curve

Using the rotating technique, start at the centre of the design and work outwards in big circles.

Dry brushing and rotating

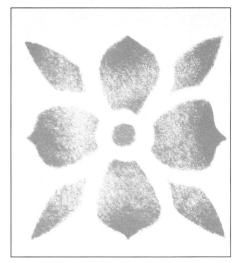

Apply a tiny amount of paint by rotating the bristles from the centre, and from the outside tips, to give more paint in these areas. Work along the line, using less pressure than on the centre and the tips. This gives a softer effect on the areas in between.

Rotating brush with leaves flicked

Fill in the petals by rotating a very dry brush and a tiny amount of paint. For the flicking effect on the leaves, use slightly more paint on the brush. Working from the centre, flick the paint outwards once or twice. Do not overdo.

Dry brushing, rotating from edge

Using big circular strokes, work from the outside of the whole stencil, moving inwards. This should leave you with more paint on the outside, as there will be less and less paint on your brush as you move inwards.

Brushing up and down from the sides

This is similar to flicking. Using slightly more paint on your brush than you would for rotating, brush up and down, then from side to side. Keep the brushmarks vertical and horizontal to give a lined effect.

Rough stippling

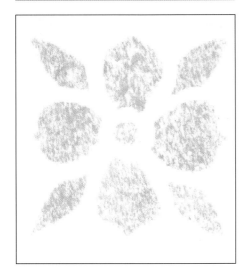

This method uses more paint and less pressure than rotating or flicking. Taking a reasonable amount of paint on the bristles of your brush, simply place it down lightly. This gives a rougher look. Do not go over it too many times as this spoils the effect.

Two-colour stippling

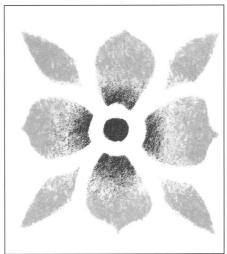

Use less paint than for rough stippling. The second colour is stippled out from the centre, to blend with the first colour.

One-sided stippling

Apply the lighter colour first, up to a point just past the centre. Apply the darker colour, and stipple to the centre. Always start on the outer edge so that you leave more paint on the edges of the stencil design.

Stippling with a dry brush

This is similar to stippling, except that it is essential to dab most of the paint off the bristles before you start. This gives a softer stippling effect.

Gentle stippling from the edges

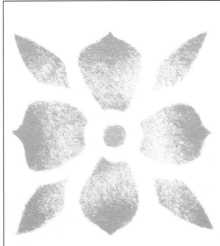

Using a very dry brush (dab most of the paint off the bristles before you start), stipple from the outside, working inwards. By the time you get to the centre, there should be hardly any paint left on your brush, ensuring a very soft paint effect in this area.

Stippling to shade with two colours

Using a reasonable amount of paint, apply the lighter shade first. Apply the darker shade to one side only of each window. (Here, the second colour is applied to the right-hand side.) A few dabs of the darker colour paint will be quite sufficient.

Flicking upwards with the brush

Using a reasonable amount of paint (not too wet or too dry) on your brush, flick upwards only. This creates a line at the top of the petals and leaves.

Flicking in two directions, up and down

Using a reasonable amount of paint on your brush, flick up and down. Do not use too much paint as it will collect on the edges of the petals and leaves.

Flicking from the outside to the centre

Using a reasonable amount of paint on your brush, flick from the outside edges in to the centre of the design. Flick from the top to the centre, from the bottom to the centre, from the left to the centre, and from the right to the centre.

Flicking from the top to the centre

Using a reasonable amount of paint on your brush, flick from the top edge of the window to the centre of the design, then from the bottom edge of the window to the centre.

Drop shadow, using a block effect

Apply the first colour, which should be the lighter shade, using a block effect. Concentrate on one side of each window (here, the right-hand side). Move the stencil slightly to the left – a few millimetres is sufficient – taking care not to move it up or down. Block again, using a darker colour, to create a drop shadow effect.

TIPS

Check the amount of paint on the stencil brush by practising on a piece of scrap paper. Excess paint can be removed by dabbing the brush on an old saucer or clean cotton cloth.

Clean the stencil brush before using a different colour to keep the colours fresh. It is a good idea to invest in several different-sized brushes.

If you want to use a different colour scheme to that shown in the project, for example to suit your existing decor, see Working with Colour earlier in this section for advice and inspiration.

Finally, do not aim for perfectly identical stencilled motifs. Much of the appeal of stencilling lies in its handpainted look and irregularities.

STAMPING TECHNIQUES

Stamping is a quick and effective method of repeating a design on a wide variety of surfaces, using many different mixtures of paints and inks. Ready-made stamps are widely available, usually mounted on wooden blocks, but they are also easy to make yourself using foam or sponge.

MAKING STAMPS

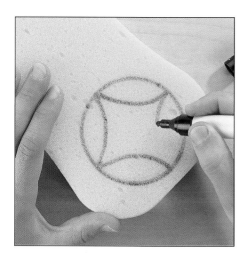

1 Use high-density sponge to create sharply defined and detailed designs. Trace your chosen motif using a soft pencil to give dark, clear lines.

2 Roughly cut around the design, then spray the piece of tracing paper with adhesive to hold it in place on the sponge while you are cutting it out.

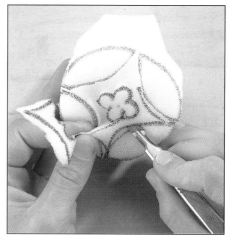

3 Cut along the outline of the motif using a craft knife, then, pinching the background sections, cut them away holding the blade away from your fingers.

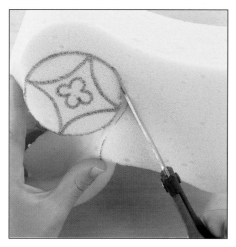

4 The surface of low-density sponge is too soft to use tracing paper as a guide for cutting out the stamp. It is easier to draw the design straight on to the sponge using a felt-tipped pen.

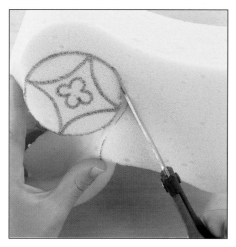

5 Sharp scissors can be used to cut out stamps made from low-density sponge and they are especially useful for cutting out the basic shapes of the motif.

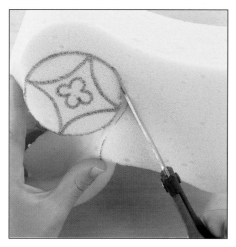

6 As with high-density sponge, the unwanted background areas should be cut away with a craft knife when the outline has been cut, but care is needed as this sponge will tear more easily. Rinse the completed stamp to remove the remains of the felt-tipped pen ink.

PAINT MIXTURES

Wallpaper paste and emulsion paint

Add 50 per cent paste to the emulsion (latex) paint to give a watercolour effect without producing a mixture that is too runny to work with. Apply the mixture using a roller, sponge or paintbrush, or dip the stamp into the paint on a flat plate.

Wallpaper paste and ink

Wallpaper paste thickens the texture of ink, while keeping the rich colour. The effect produced depends on the proportion of ink in the mixture. It will give a more even spread of colour than using emulsion (latex). Apply using a roller or paintbrush.

Varnish and emulsion paint

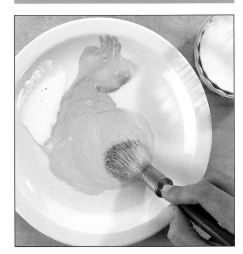

The density of the emulsion (latex) paint is diluted as with wallpaper paste, but this can also be used to create different sheens according to the type of varnish used. Apply with a roller, paintbrush or sponge, or dip the stamp into the paint on a plate.

Varnish and ink

This effect is similar to the wallpaper paste mixture, but creates a smoother mix as both materials are fine in texture. Again, different sheens can be obtained depending on the varnish used. Apply with a roller.

Wallpaper paste and woodstain

The wallpaper paste dilutes the colour density of the woodstain while thickening the mixture for ease of use. Use quick-drying, water-based woodstains, which are available in a range of colours. Apply with a roller.

Interior filler and emulsion paint

This mixture thickens the paint as opposed to diluting the colour, and is good for creating relief effects. Apply the mixture generously, using a paintbrush, or dip the stamp into the paint on a plate.

HOW TO APPLY PAINT

Using a roller

Pour a little paint on to the side of a flat plate, then, using a small sponge roller, pick up a small amount of paint and roll it out over the rest of the plate until you have an even covering. Roll the paint on to the stamp.

Using a paintbrush

Use a fairly stiff brush and apply the paint with a dabbing or stippling motion. This technique enables more than one colour to be applied and for detail to be picked out. Be careful not to overload the stamp, as this may cause it to slip when stamping.

Dipping into paint on a plate

Brush a thin coat of paint on to a flat plate, then press the stamp into the paint. You may need to do this several times to get an even coating. Initially the stamp will absorb a good amount of paint. Keep brushing more paint on to the plate as you work.

Using a roller and brush

Use a sponge roller to apply the paint evenly over the whole stamp. Use a brush to apply a second colour to act as a highlight or shadow, or to pick out details of the design.

Using a sponge

Spread an even coating of paint on a plate, then use a natural sponge to pick up the paint and dab it on to the stamp. This method allows you to put a light, even covering of paint on to the stamp.

Using an inkpad

Press the stamp lightly on to the inkpad. You may need to do this several times to ensure a good covering. It is difficult to overload the stamp using inkpads. This technique will give a dry look to the stamped motifs.

PREPARING SURFACES

Tiles, china and glass

These are all prepared in the same way, using soapy water to remove dirt and grease, then drying with a lint-free cloth. Appropriate special paints, such as enamel or ceramic paints, must be used as normal emulsion (latex) and acrylic paints will not adhere well and are not sufficiently durable for these surfaces. It is often necessary to strengthen the finished design by applying a coat of varnish.

1 Wash the tile or glass with soapy water and rinse thoroughly. To remove any remaining traces of grease, give the surface a final wipe with a cloth dipped in methylated spirits (methyl alcohol) and leave to dry.

2 When printing on a curved surface, carefully roll the stamp while holding the object securely. Sponge stamps are best suited for this purpose. Rubber stamps are less suitable.

Fabrics

Fabrics must be washed and ironed before stamping to remove any dressing and allow for any shrinkage. Use special fabric paint or ink so that the item can be washed after stamping. Fix the paint to the fabric according to the manufacturer's instructions.

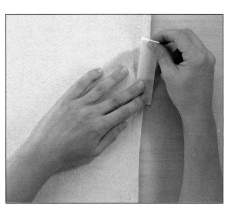

1 Once ironed, lay the fabric on a flat surface and tape down the edges to hold it firmly in position.

2 Place a piece of card (stock) or scrap paper under the area to be stamped to stop any of the paint bleeding through the fabric.

Wood

Wood should be lightly sanded before stamping and varnished afterwards. New wood should be sealed with a coat of shellac to stop resin leaking through the grain. When using woodstains, keep the stamp quite dry to stop the stain bleeding into the grain of the wood.

1 Sand the surface of the wood, then wipe down with a soft cloth to remove any loose dust.

2 Once dry, the stamped design can be rubbed back with abrasive paper to create a distressed effect.

PLANNING A DESIGN

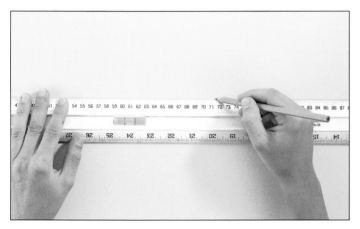

1 With the aid of a spirit level, draw a faint pencil line to use as a guide when stamping.

2 Stamp the motif several times on scrap paper and cut out the prints. Tape them to the wall so that you can judge how your design will look.

3 When using a stamp mounted on a block, you can draw a straight line on the back to help with positioning. Align the block with the pencil guideline on the wall.

4 A piece of card (stock) held between the previous print and the stamp will ensure that there is consistent spacing between the motifs.

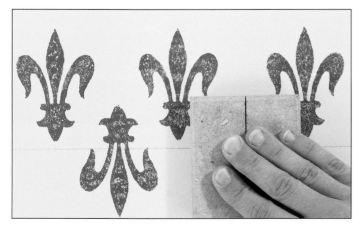

5 For a tighter design, butt the stamped motifs together without any spacing.

6 Once the paint is dry, the pencil guideline can be removed using a clean cloth wrung out in soapy water and rubbed along the line.

STAMP EFFECTS

Although basic stamping is a very simple and straightforward technique, you can achieve many different and subtle effects with stamps, depending on the paint mixture you use and the way in which it is applied. The same stamp, cut from high-density sponge, was used to make all the following prints.

Half-shade

Roll the first, paler colour over the stamp, then roll a second, darker shade over one half only, to create a three-dimensional shadowed effect.

Two-tone

Using a paintbrush, load the stamp with the first colour, then apply the second colour to the top and bottom edges only.

Two-tone with dry roller

For an even subtler colour mix, roll the second colour right over the first using a very dry roller.

Contrasting detail

To pick out details of the design in a contrasting colour, apply the first colour with a roller, then use a paintbrush to apply the second contrasting colour in the areas you want.

Partial outline

This shadow effect is produced by stamping the motif in one colour, then partially outlining the print using a paintbrush or felt-tip pen. For a natural shadow effect, place all the shadow on either the right-hand or left-hand side.

Drop shadow

Another, very subtle, effect of shadows and highlights can be produced by stamping the motif in the darker colour first. When this is dry, load the stamp with the paler colour and print over the first image, positioning the stamp slightly to one side.

Stippled

This stippled effect gives the stamped print lots of surface interest. Apply the paint with a stiff paintbrush and a dabbing, stippling motion.

Wallpaper paste

Adding wallpaper paste to emulsion (latex) paint gives the stamped print a translucent, watercolour quality.

Light shadow

Here the paint has been applied with a roller, covering each element of the motif more heavily on one side to create a delicate shadow effect.

Second print

After loading the stamp with paint, print first on a piece of scrap paper. This very delicate image is the second print.

Sponge print

Apply a sponge print in one colour over a rollered colour in another colour for a different effect, as shown here.

Distressed

A single colour of paint applied with a dry roller produces an aged, distressed paint effect.

THE PROJECTS

This section of the book puts each of the painting, stencilling and stamping techniques into practice, with original ideas for every room of the house. There are projects suitable for decorating large areas quickly, involving colourwashing and using a roller, and more complex projects that make use of intricate stamps and stencils. You will be surprised at how quickly you can transform even a very large surface with a striking pattern. Classic lines and stripes never seem to go out of fashion, and stencils and stamps can add an individual touch to your schemes. Refer to the templates at the back of the book for some of the more complicated designs.

ABOVE: A simple sandcastle stencil is given extra vitality with handpainted flagpoles.

LEFT: This Renaissance wall design can be achieved by using a combination of ornate stencils and rich paint colours.

ROUGH PLASTER COLOURWASH

This sunny yellow wall was given a rough-textured look by trowelling on a ready-mixed medium (joint compound), available from do-it-yourself stores, which is normally used for smoothing walls and ceilings that have unwanted texture. Colourwashing in two shades of yellow gives added depth and tone. The absorbent wall surface picks up varying degrees of paint, and there will be some areas which are not coloured at all, but this is all part of the attractive rural effect.

1 Apply the coating medium (joint compound) to the wall, using a plasterer's trowel or large scraper. You can decide whether to have a very rough effect or a smoother finish. Leave to dry overnight.

2 Using a large decorator's paintbrush, paint the wall with two coats of white emulsion (latex), leaving each coat of paint to dry thoroughly.

3 Dilute one shade of yellow paint with about 75 per cent water. Dip a damp sponge into the paint and wipe it over the wall, using plenty of arm movement as though you were cleaning it.

4 Leave the first shade of yellow paint to dry. Dilute the second shade of yellow paint with about 75 per cent water and wipe it over the first colour in the same way.

DIAMOND-STENCILLED WALL

H̲ere a stunning colour scheme is created by dragging a deep green glaze over a lime
green base. The surface is then stencilled with shiny aluminium leaf diamonds,
which stand out against the strong background. This paint finish would look very dramatic
in a dining room, with muted lighting used to catch the metallic diamond highlights.

You will need

- 2 large decorator's paintbrushes
- emulsion (latex) paint in lime green
- artist's acrylic paint in monestial green
  and emerald green
- acrylic scumble
- pencil
- stencil card (stock)
- craft knife
- cutting mat or thick card (stock)
- 2 artist's paintbrushes
- acrylic size
- aluminium leaf
- make-up brush
- clear shellac and brush

1 Using one of the large decorator's brushes, paint the wall with lime green
emulsion (latex) paint. Leave to dry.

2 Mix a glaze from 1 part monestial
green acrylic paint, 1 part emerald
green acrylic paint and 6 parts acrylic
scumble. Paint the glaze on to the wall
with random brushstrokes.

3 Working quickly with a dry large
decorator's brush, go over the
surface using long, downward strokes.
Overlap the strokes and don't stop
mid-stroke. Leave to dry.

▶

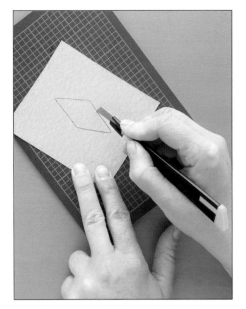

4 Draw a small diamond shape in pencil on to stencil card (stock). Cut out the shape, using a craft knife and cutting mat or thick card.

5 Using an artist's paintbrush, apply a thin, even coat of acrylic size through the stencil card on to the wall. Repeat the diamond motif as many times as desired to make a decorative pattern.

6 After about 20 minutes, touch the size lightly with a finger to check that it has become tacky. If not, wait a little longer. Press a piece of aluminium leaf gently on to the size.

7 Working carefully, peel off the aluminium leaf, then brush off the excess with the make-up brush.

8 Using the second artist's paintbrush, apply clear shellac over the diamond motifs. Leave to dry.

LIMEWASHED WALL

For an instant limewashed effect, apply white emulsion (latex) paint over a darker base with a dry brush, then remove some of the paint with a cloth soaked in methylated spirits (methyl alcohol). This is a good way to decorate uneven or damaged walls, and gives a pleasing rustic effect.

You will need

- matt emulsion (flat latex) paint in cream and white
- 2 large decorator's paintbrushes
- clean cotton cloths
- methylated spirits (methyl alcohol)
- neutral wax

1 Paint the wall with a coat of cream matt emulsion (flat latex) paint, using one of the large decorator's brushes. Leave to dry.

2 Using the second decorator's brush, dip the tip of the dry paintbrush into the white emulsion paint. Using random strokes, dry brush the paint on to the wall. Leave to dry.

3 Using a cloth, rub methylated spirits (methyl alcohol) into the wall in some areas. This will remove some of the paint, giving a natural weathered effect. Leave to dry.

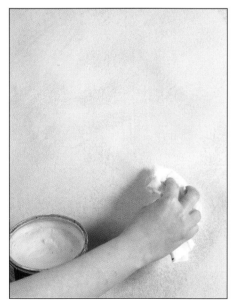

4 Using a clean cloth, rub wax all over the wall to seal the paint and protect the surface.

MISTY LILAC STRIPES

Here, wide stripes are painted and the wet paint dabbed with mutton cloth (stockinet) to soften the effect and blend in brushmarks. As an extra touch, paint a triangle at the top of each stripe. If you do not have a picture rail, take the stripes up to the top of the wall and place the triangles along the skirting (base) board.

1 Paint the walls with white satin-finish emulsion (latex) paint, using a paint roller and tray. Mark the centre of the most important wall, below the picture rail (if you have one), with a pencil. Make marks 7.5cm/3in either side of this, then every 15cm/6in. Continue making 15cm/6in marks around the room until the marks meet at the least noticeable corner.

2 Hang a short length of plumbline from one of the marks, and mark with a dot where it rests. Hang the plumbline from this dot and mark where it rests. Continue down the wall. Repeat for each mark below the picture rail.

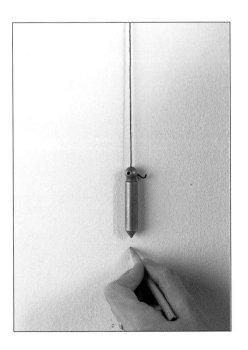

3 Starting in the centre of the wall, place strips of masking tape either side of the marked row of dots to give a 15cm/6in wide stripe. Repeat for the other rows of dots.

4 Dilute some of the lilac paint with about 25 per cent water and 25 per cent acrylic scumble. Brush on to a section of the first stripe. Complete each stripe in two or three stages, depending on the height of the room, blending the joins to get an even result.

5 Dab the wet paint lightly with a mutton cloth (stockinet) to smooth out the brushmarks. Complete all the stripes, then carefully peel away the masking tape and leave the paint to dry.

6 Cut a card (stock) triangle with a 15cm/6in base and measuring 10cm/4in from the base to the tip. Use this as a template to mark the centre of each of the stripes, lilac and white, 10cm/4in below the picture rail.

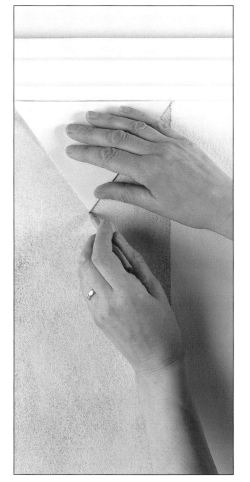

7 Working on one stripe at a time, place strips of masking tape between the top corners of the stripe and the marked dot, as shown.

8 Brush on the lilac paint mix, then dab the mutton cloth over the wet paint as before. Leave the paint to dry. Repeat for all the stripes.

9 Dilute some lilac paint with about 20 parts water. Brush over the wall in all directions to give a hint of colour to the white stripes.

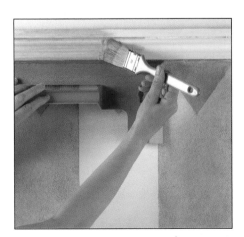

10 Add a little paint to the remaining diluted mixture to strengthen the colour. Using a paint guard or strip of card to protect the painted wall, brush the paint on to the picture rail.

RED-PANELLED WALL

This bright red wall has been beautifully toned down with a translucent glaze of deep maroon acrylic paint mixed with scumble. The panel has been given a very simple trompe l'oeil treatment, using dark and light shades of paint to create a 3-D effect.

You will need

- satin-finish emulsion (latex) paint in bright red
- medium and small decorator's paintbrushes
- ruler and pencil
- spirit level
- plumbline
- masking tape
- craft knife
- artist's acrylic paint in deep maroon, black and white
- acrylic scumble
- mutton cloth (stockinet)
- clean cotton cloth
- coarse-grade abrasive paper

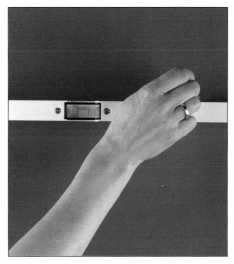

1 Paint the wall with two coats of bright red paint, leaving each coat to dry. Mark the centre top of the panel. Draw a horizontal line 30cm/12in either side of this mark.

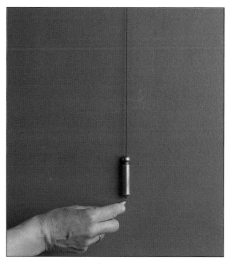

2 Drop a plumbline 90cm/36in down from each end of the drawn line and make a mark. Draw a line between all the marked points to give a 60 × 90cm/24 × 36in panel.

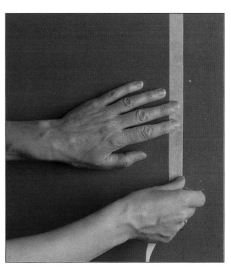

3 Place strips of masking tape around the outer edge of the panel. Neaten the corners where the strips of tape meet with a craft knife.

4 Mix the maroon paint with acrylic scumble to the required colour. Brush this on to the panel.

▶

5 Immediately dab a mutton cloth (stockinet) over the wet glaze to even out the texture. Leave the glaze to dry.

6 Starting in a corner, brush the maroon glaze on to a section of the wall, roughly the same size as the panel. Dab it with the mutton cloth to blend the brushmarks as before, stopping just short of the edge of the panel. Roll up the cotton cloth into a sausage shape and then immediately roll it over the wet glaze, changing direction to give a more random effect. Leave the glaze to dry. Repeat all over the rest of the wall.

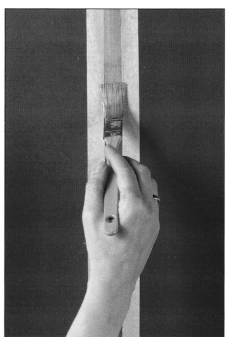

7 Remove the masking tape. Place new strips of tape either side of the bright red line now revealed and trim the corners with the craft knife. Mix a small amount of black acrylic paint with some of the maroon glaze. Brush this between the masking tape down one side of the panel, on the side where the light source is. Place a piece of coarse-grade abrasive paper diagonally at the top and clean off the glaze that extends beyond. Keeping the abrasive paper in the same position, repeat on the top border of the panel.

8 Add a small amount of white acrylic paint to the maroon glaze and apply to the remaining two borders in the same way. Leave to dry, then carefully remove the masking tape.

TWO-TONE ROLLERED WALL

For this quick, ingenious paint effect, two shades of emulsion (latex) are placed next to each other in a paint tray and then rollered on to the wall together. Moving the roller in different directions blends the paint very effectively.

1 Using a paint roller, paint the wall with a base coat of cream emulsion (latex). Leave to dry.

2 Pour the yellow and the terracotta emulsion into the paint tray together, half on each side. The two colours of paint will sit side by side without mixing.

3 Paint the wall, applying the roller at a variety of different angles to blend the two colours.

4 When complete, roller over the wall a few times to blend the paint further, but don't overwork.

OTHER COLOURS

ABOVE: *Alternative colours – yellow and cream emulsion (latex) over a dark turquoise base coat.*

ABOVE: *Complementary colours – light and mid-blue emulsion (latex) over a pale green base coat.*

STONE WALL

A subtle stone effect is created using several different techniques. Layers of paint are built up by stippling, sponging and rubbing colours on and off, and a hog softening brush is used to blend the wet glazes to look like stone. The wall is divided by a trompe l'oeil dado (chair) rail.

You will need

- large decorator's paintbrush
- emulsion (latex) paint in cream
- spirit level
- ruler
- pencil
- masking tape
- acrylic paint in raw umber, white and yellow ochre
- acrylic scumble
- decorator's block brush or stippling brush
- natural sponge
- hog softening brush
- clean cotton cloths
- fine artist's paintbrush

1 Using a large decorator's paintbrush, paint the wall with cream emulsion (latex). Leave to dry.

2 Using a level and ruler, draw pencil lines 6.5cm/2½in apart at dado (chair) rail height.

3 Place masking tape inside the two pencil lines, smoothing it in place with your fingers.

4 Mix a glaze of 1 part raw umber acrylic paint to 6 parts scumble. Stipple this on to the wall, using the tip of the decorator's block brush or stippling brush. Do not stipple over the masked area. Leave to dry.

5 Mix a glaze with the white acrylic paint in the same way. Dampen a sponge and apply the glaze over the stippling, varying your hand position to avoid a uniform effect.

6 Using a hog softening brush, skim gently over the surface of the white glaze while it is still wet.

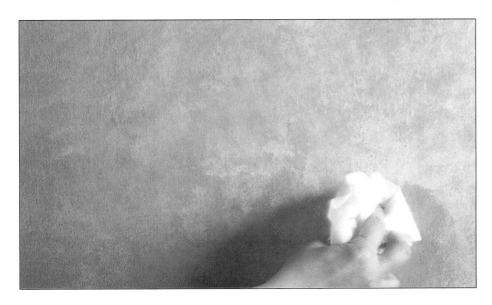

7 Mix a glaze with the yellow ochre paint as in step 4, but this time rub it into the wall with a cloth. Leave some areas of white glaze showing.

8 Using another dampened cloth, rub some areas to disperse the paint. Leave to dry.

9 Using a pencil and ruler, draw in the main lines of the false dado rail. Follow the illustration or copy a piece of moulding.

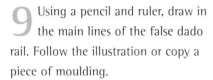

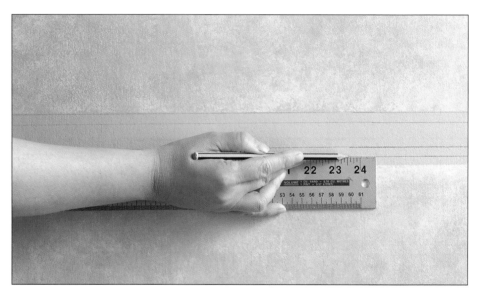

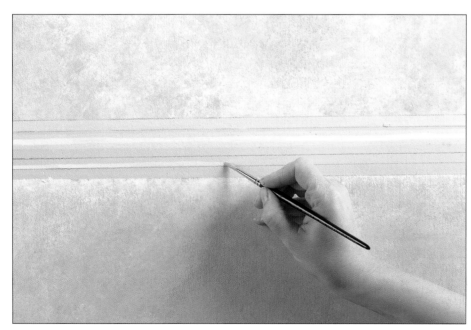

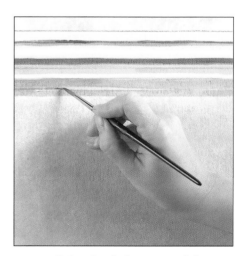

11 Paint the darker areas of the trompe l'oeil dado rail in raw umber acrylic paint. Leave to dry. Mix a little white acrylic paint into the raw umber and then add the softer, shadowed areas.

10 Highlight the pencil lines in white acrylic paint, using a fine artist's paintbrush. Leave to dry.

MAKING SANDCASTLES

Evocative of childhood summers spent on the beach, sandcastles are simple, colourful shapes to stencil. Perfect for a child's room or for a family bathroom, they will bring a touch of humour to your walls. Paint the flags in different colours or glue on paper flags for added interest.

1 Paint below dado (chair) rail height in blue emulsion (latex). When dry, rub on white emulsion with a sponge. Trace the template at the back of the book. Cut the stencils from acetate as described in Stencilling Techniques.

2 Using a tape measure, measure the wall to calculate how many sandcastles you can fit on and make light pencil marks at regular intervals. Hold the stencil above the dado rail centred on one of the marked points and secure the corners with masking tape.

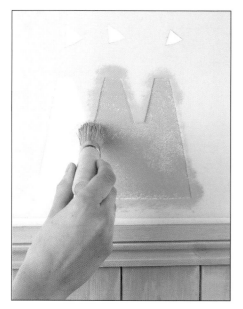

3 Using yellow stencil paint and a stencil brush, stencil in the base of the first sandcastle.

4 Using a smaller stencil brush, paint each of the three flags in a different colour of your choice. Carefully remove the stencil from the wall.

5 When the paint has dried, stencil a star on the sandcastle in a contrasting colour of paint. Try to alternate the colour of the star for each sandcastle on the wall.

6 Using a fine artist's paintbrush and black stencil paint, paint in the flagpoles. The lines do not need to be straight: wavy lines will add to the quality of the finished project.

7 Continue stencilling the sandcastles along the wall using your pencil marks to position them.

8 As an alternative to stencilling the flags, cut out triangles of coloured paper and glue them to the wall with PVA (white) glue, then paint in the flagpoles.

ABOVE: *Don't be too exacting when hand painting the flagpoles. Wobbly lines and erratic angles add to the childlike and spontaneous quality of the sandcastle frieze.*

LEFT: *As a variation on the holiday theme, you could cover the wall above the dado (chair) rail with tropical shapes in Caribbean colours. Paint the wall first in a strong background colour.*

PENNSYLVANIA-DUTCH TULIPS

This American folk-art inspired idea uses the rich colours and simple motifs beloved by the German and Dutch immigrants to Pennsylvania. Create the effect of hand-painted wallpaper or, for a beginner's project, take a single motif and use it to decorate a small cabinet.

You will need

- emulsion (latex) paint in dark ochre
- large and small decorator's paintbrushes
- woodwash in indigo blue and mulberry
- stencil card (stock)
- craft knife and self-healing cutting mat
- pencil
- ruler
- stencil brushes
- stencil paint in red, light green, dark green and pale brown
- saucer or cloth
- artist's paintbrush

1 Dilute 1 part dark ochre emulsion (latex) with 1 part water. Using a large paintbrush, cover the top half of the wall with the diluted paint. Use vertical brushstrokes for an even texture.

2 Paint the lower half of the wall with indigo blue woodwash. Finish off with a curving line using a dry brush to suggest woodgrain.

3 Paint the dado (chair) rail or a strip at dado rail height in mulberry woodwash, using a narrow brush to give a clean edge.

5 Dip a stencil brush into red stencil paint. Rub the brush on a saucer or cloth until it is almost dry before stencilling in the tulip flowers. Leave to dry.

4 Trace the tulip and heart templates at the back of the book and cut the stencils from stencil card (stock) as described in Stencilling Techniques. Mark the centre of each edge of the stencil. Measure the wall and divide it into equal sections, so that the repeats will fall at about 20cm/8in intervals. Mark the positions with pencil, so that they can be rubbed out later.

6 Paint the leaves in light green stencil paint with dark green shading, using an artist's paintbrush. Paint the stems in dark green. Leave to dry.

7 Stencil the basket in pale brown stencil paint using a chunky stencil brush to give texture.

▶

8 Stencil a single heart between each two baskets of tulips using red stencil paint. Judge the positioning of the hearts by eye to give a natural handpainted look.

ABOVE: Decorate a matching key cabinet following the same method and using a single motif.

ABOVE: A simple tulip motif stencilled kitchen storage tin gives instant folk-art style.

RENAISSANCE ART

Turn your hallway into a dramatic entrance with ornate stencils and rich colours. Combine them with gold accessories, antique furniture and velvets and braids to complete the theatrical setting. This design would also be ideal for creating an intimate dining room for candlelit dinners.

1 Using a ruler and spirit level, divide the wall in half horizontally with a pencil line, then draw a second line 15cm/6in above the first. Stick a line of masking tape just below this top line. Dilute 1 part slate-blue emulsion (latex) with 1 part water and colour the top half of the wall using a sponge.

2 Stick masking tape above the bottom pencil line. Dilute 1 part terracotta emulsion with 1 part water. Sponge over the lower half of the wall.

3 Sponge lightly over the terracotta sponging with pale slate-blue to add a textural effect. Remove the strips of masking tape.

4 Colour the centre band with diluted peach emulsion using a stencil brush. Trace the templates at the back of the book and cut out the stencils from stencil card (stock) using a craft knife and self-healing cutting mat.

5 Stencil the wall motifs at roughly regular intervals over the upper part of the wall, using dark grey-blue stencil paint. Rotate the stencil with every alternate motif to give movement to the design.

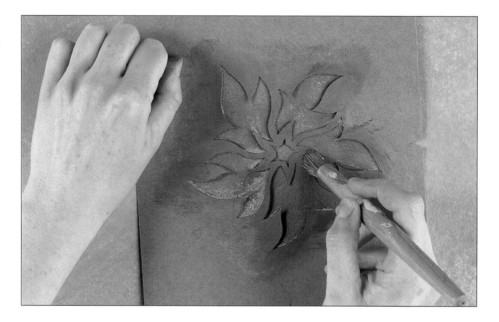

6 Starting at the right-hand side of the peach band, stencil the border motif with terracotta stencil paint. Add details in emerald and turquoise. Continue along the wall, positioning the stencil beside the previous motif so that the spaces are equal.

OPPOSITE: *Make a matching patchwork cushion cover with pieces of fabric stencilled with gold fabric paint. Add offcuts of velvet and cover all the seams with ornate trimmings.*

THROUGH THE GRAPEVINE

This classic grape stencil will bring back holiday memories of sipping wine under a canopy of vines. The stencilled grapes are all the more effective set against the purple and green dry-brushed walls. Practise your paint effects on small pieces of board before tackling full-scale walls.

1 Dip the end of a large paintbrush in purple emulsion (latex), scrape off the excess and apply to the wall, brushing in varying directions and not completely covering the wall. This process is known as dry-brushing.

2 Repeat the dry-brushing process with green emulsion, filling in some of the bare areas and going over the purple paint.

3 Draw a horizontal pencil line at the desired height on the wall using a ruler and spirit level.

4 Trace the grape stencil at the back of the book and cut the stencil from acetate. Tape the stencil in place with its top edge on the pencil line. Apply purple stencil paint over the whole stencil.

5 Add lilac stencil paint at the bottom of each window in the stencil to create the effect of highlights on the grapes. Repeat the stencil along the wall to create a frieze.

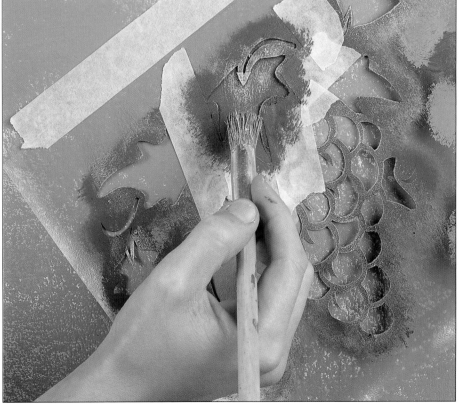

6 Dip the stencil brush in the silver gilt cream, brush off any excess and brush over the stencils using an up and down movement.

7 Select a few leaf shapes from the stencil and mask them off. Position the leaves randomly over the wall and stencil in purple. Brush over with the gilt cream using the same technique as before.

8 Leave the stencilling to dry overnight. With a soft cotton cloth, buff up the silver gilt cream to a shine. A single stencil would also work well on a cabinet panel or table top.

ROPE AND SHELLS

The chunky rope cleverly linking the seashells is echoed by individual stencilled knots. Shells are always popular motifs for a bathroom design and look good in many colour combinations, from nautical blue and white to greens and aquas or pinks and corals.

1 Using a household sponge rub nautical blue emulsion (latex) paint over the wall to create a very rough and patchy finish. Leave to dry.

2 Using a clean sponge, rub a generous amount of white emulsion over the wall so that it almost covers the blue, giving a slightly mottled effect.

3 Using a ruler and spirit level, draw a horizontal pencil line at the desired height of the border. Trace the templates at the back of the book and cut the stencils from acetate. Position the seashore stencil with its top edge on the pencil line and secure with masking tape. Stencil dark blue stencil paint around the edges of the shells and seaweed, using a stencil brush.

4 Using light blue stencil paint, shade in the centre of the shells, the seaweed and the recesses of the rope.

5 Using camel stencil paint, fill in the remainder of the rope and then lightly highlight the shells and seaweed. Continue to stencil the shell and rope border right around the room.

6 Draw a vertical line from each loop of rope to the skirting (base) board. Starting 30cm/12in from the stencilled border, make pencil marks at 30cm/12in intervals down the line to mark the positions of the rope knots. Start every alternate line of marks 15cm/6in below the border so that the knots will be staggered.

8 Stencil the remainder of the rope in camel. Leave to dry. Remove any visible pencil marks with an eraser and wipe over with a slightly damp cloth.

7 Tape the knotted rope stencil on to the first pencil mark. Stencil dark blue stencil paint in the recesses of the rope.

LEFT: *Create a variation on the sea theme by stencilling a simple row of starfish at dado (chair) rail height. The starfish motif is repeated on the chair seat to give a pleasing coordinated look.*

HERALDIC DINING ROOM

Lend an atmosphere of medieval luxury to your dining room with richly coloured walls and heraldic motifs stencilled in the same deep tones. Gilt accessories, heavy fabrics and a profusion of candles team well with this decor. All that remains is to prepare a sumptuous banquet.

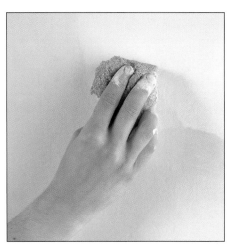

1 Using a large household sponge, rub camel emulsion (latex) all over the wall. Leave to dry.

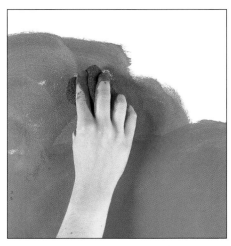

2 Repeat using a generous amount of deep red emulsion so that it almost covers the camel, giving a slightly mottled effect. Leave to dry.

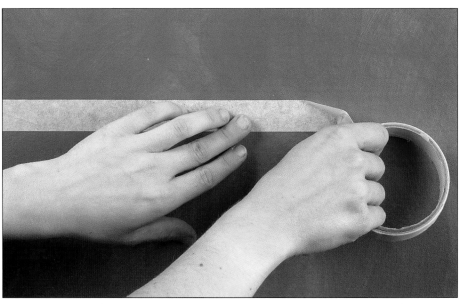

3 Using a ruler and spirit level, draw a pencil line at dado (chair) rail height. Stick a line of masking tape just above it.

4 Sponge deep purple emulsion all over the wall below the masking tape to give a slightly mottled effect. Leave to dry, then remove the masking tape.

5 Trace the heraldic templates at the back of the book and cut the stencils from acetate. Secure the rose stencil above the dividing line with strips of masking tape. Stencil in purple emulsion, using the stencil brush. When dry, position the fleur-de-lys stencil next to the rose and stencil in camel emulsion. Continue to alternate the stencils around the room.

6 Place the highlight stencils over the painted motifs and, with a stencil brush, add purple details to the camel fleurs-de-lys and camel details to the purple roses as shown.

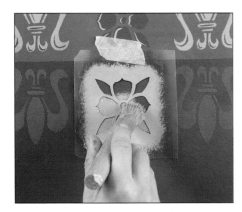

7 Flip the stencils over and position as mirror images below the previously stencilled motifs. Stencil the roses in camel, and the fleurs-de-lys in red.

8 Add highlights as before, using camel on the red fleurs-de-lys, and purple on the camel roses.

9 Using a fine lining brush and camel paint, paint a narrow line where the red and purple paints meet. If you do not have the confidence to do this freehand, position two rows of masking tape on the wall, leaving a small gap in between. When the line of paint is dry, carefully remove the masking tape.

CELESTIAL CHERUBS

This exuberant baroque decoration is perfect for a sumptuous bedroom. The cherubs are stencilled in metallic shades of bronze, gold and copper, but you could use plain colours for a simpler result that would be suitable for a child's room.

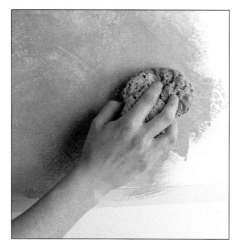

1 Paint the wall with white emulsion (latex). Dilute 1 part blue emulsion with 1 part water, and, using a sponge, lightly apply it to the wall.

2 Sponge in a few areas of grey to give the impression of a cloudy sky. Sponge in a few pale areas by mixing a little white into the grey paint to suggest the edges of clouds.

3 Trace the cherub and heart templates at the back of the book and cut the stencils from stencil card (stock). Secure the cherub stencil to the wall with masking tape. Stencil the body of the cherub in gold stencil paint.

4 Stencil the cherub's wings and bow in copper stencil paint, covering the adjacent parts of the stencil with a piece of scrap paper.

5 Stencil the cherub's hair and arrow in bronze stencil paint, again protecting the adjacent areas with scrap paper.

6 Stencil the drape in white stencil paint. Add some bronze shadows to the folds of the drape.

7 To give a three-dimensional effect to the whole design, add bronze shadows at the edges of various parts of the cherub motif. Follow the shading shown in the photograph below.

8 Stencil more cherubs, varying the design by reversing the card sometimes. Stencil the interlinked hearts in the spaces using bronze stencil paint.

LEFT: Try to position the stencils so that the cupids are aiming their arrows at the interlinked hearts – a perfect theme for a romantic bedroom.

FLOWER POT FRIEZE

This witty frieze has a 1950s feel and creates an eye-catching feature above a half-boarded wall. Use scraps of left-over wallpaper or sheets of wrapping paper for the pots, then stamp an exuberant display of flowers to go inside them.

You will need

- matt emulsion (flat latex) paint in pale blue and white
- 2 large decorator's paintbrushes
- clean cotton cloth
- pencil
- wallpaper or wrapping paper
- scissors
- PVA (white) glue and brush
- acrylic paint in green
- fine artist's paintbrush
- stamp inkpads in a variety of colours
- large and small daisy rubber stamps
- cotton wool buds (swabs)
- scrap paper

1 Paint the tongue-and-groove boarding or the lower half of the wall with pale blue emulsion (latex) paint. Leave to dry.

2 Using a dry paintbrush, lightly brush white emulsion over the flat colour. For a softer effect, rub the paint in with a cotton cloth.

3 To make the frieze, draw flower-pot shapes on to scraps of different wallpapers or wrapping paper and cut them out. Cut scalloped strips of paper and glue one along the top of each flower pot, using PVA (white) glue.

4 Glue the flower pots along the wall, at evenly spaced intervals. Alternate the different papers to create a pleasing random effect.

5 Using acrylic paint and a fine artist's paintbrush, paint green stems coming out of each pot. Leave the paint to dry before beginning to print the flowers.

7 Test the daisy stamps on a sheet of scrap paper before applying them to the wall.

6 Use coloured inkpads to ink the daisy stamps, using the lighter colours first. To ink the flower centre in a different colour, remove the first colour from the centre using a cottonwool bud (swab), then use a small inkpad to dab on the second colour.

▶

8 Print the lighter-coloured flowers on the ends of some of the stems, using both the large and small daisy stamps. Allow the ink to dry.

9 Print darker flowers on the remaining stems. Allow the flowers to overlap to create full, blossoming pots.

MOORISH TILE EFFECT

Moorish wall patterns are based on abstract, geometric motifs which you can reproduce most effectively with stamps. In this wall treatment, a lozenge shape is incorporated in a subtle tile design on a cool colourwashed background.

You will need

- matt emulsion (flat latex) paint in mid-blue, off-white and terracotta
- wallpaper paste
- paint-mixing container
- Large and small decorator's paintbrushes
- thin card (stock)
- ruler
- pencil
- scissors
- medium-density sponge, such as a kitchen sponge
- felt-tipped pen
- craft knife
- spirit level
- fine artist's paintbrush

1 Mix the mid-blue emulsion (latex) with 50 per cent wallpaper paste. Apply to the walls with a large paintbrush, working at random angles and blending the brushstrokes to avoid any hard edges.

2 Mix the off-white emulsion with 75 per cent wallpaper paste and brush on to the walls as before, to soften the effect. Allow to dry.

3 To make a template for the tile shape, cut out a 30cm/12in square of thin card (stock).

4 Mark the sides of the card square 5cm/2in from each corner, draw a line across the diagonal and cut off the corners.

5 Copy the template from the back of the book and transfer it to a 5cm/2in square of medium-density sponge using a felt-tipped pen. Cut away the excess sponge using a craft knife.

6 Using a spirit level, draw a horizontal line around the room where you want the top of the pattern. Place the top of the card template against the line and draw around it. Repeat all over the pattern area.

7 Use small decorator's paintbrushes to load the stamp with mid-blue and terracotta emulsion paint. Print the motif in the diamond shapes created by the template.

8 Dilute off-white emulsion with water to the consistency of thick cream. Using a fine artist's paintbrush, paint over the pencil lines.

SANTA FE LIVING ROOM

Aztec motifs such as this bird are bold, stylized and one-dimensional, and translate perfectly into stamps. Strong colour contrasts suit this style, but here the pattern is confined to widely spaced stripes over a cool white wall, and further restrained with a final light wash of white paint.

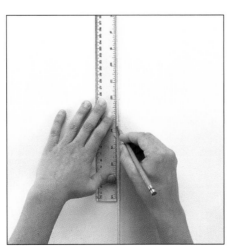

1 Dilute the off-white emulsion (latex) paint with 50 per cent water and apply a wash over the walls using a sponge, alternating the angle at which you work. Allow to dry.

2 Using a large, dry brush, apply warm white emulsion to some areas to achieve a rough-looking surface. Allow to dry.

3 Starting 10cm/4in from one corner, and using a plumbline as a guide, draw a straight pencil line from the top to the bottom of the wall.

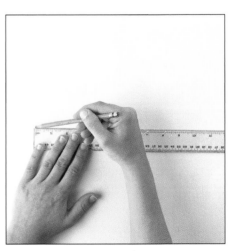

4 Measure 45cm/18in along the wall, hang the plumbline again and mark a second vertical line. Draw another line 10cm/4in away to create a band. Repeat all around the room.

5 Apply masking tape to the walls on each outer edge of the marked bands.

6 Paint the bands in deep red emulsion using a medium decorator's paintbrush. Leave to dry.

7 Draw a 10 × 20cm/4 × 8in diamond shape on to medium-density sponge. Cut out the shape using a craft knife.

8 Use a small roller to load the stamp with navy blue emulsion paint. Stamp the diamonds down the red bands, starting from the top and just touching at the tips.

9 Copy the bird template at the back of the book on to a piece of high-density sponge. Cut away the excess sponge using a craft knife.

10 Use the small roller to load the bird stamp with off-white emulsion. Print the birds upright, roughly in the centre of the diamonds. Make sure that they all face in the same direction.

11 When the bird motifs are dry, use minimal pressure and a large dry paintbrush to brush gently over each band with warm white emulsion (latex). This will soften the bold colours.

ART NOUVEAU ROSES

This stylized, flowing design is inspired by the rose motif found in the work of Charles Rennie Mackintosh, who used it repeatedly in his interior designs, on chairs, doors, leaded glass and textiles. Used here to link a chair with the wall behind it, it is equally effective as a single motif or as a repeating pattern.

You will need

- pencil
- scissors
- high-density sponge, such as upholstery foam
- craft knife and cutting mat
- ruler
- stiff card (stock)
- PVA (white) glue and brush
- felt-tipped pen
- small coin
- medium artist's paintbrush
- acrylic paint in pink and green
- director's chair with calico cover
- tailor's chalk
- fabric paint in green and pink

1 Scale up the designs at the back of the book to the size you require and make templates. Cut a square of sponge to fit the rose and a rectangle for the stem. Cut two pieces of card (stock) to fit the sponge shapes and glue them on using PVA (white) glue.

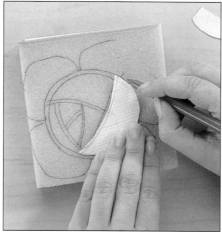

2 Using a felt-tipped pen, transfer the designs to the sponge by drawing around the templates. Mark the top of each design on the card at the back.

3 Cut away the excess sponge from around the motifs using a craft knife. Make the stamp for the small dots by drawing around a small coin and cutting it out.

4 Using a pencil and ruler, and with the large stamp as a size guide, mark the positions of the bottom edges of the roses and stems on the wall, keeping the line parallel with the dado (chair) rail. Repeat for the upper line of roses, then mark the centres of the small dots directly above the lower ones, and on a line equidistant from the two rows of roses.

5 Using a medium artist's paintbrush, load the rose stamp evenly with a quantity of pink acrylic paint.

6 Match the bottom edge of the stamp to the marked wall and apply the stamp.

7 Load the small dot stamp with green acrylic paint. Stamp dots at the marked points on the wall.

8 Load the stem stamp with green paint and stamp at the marked points. Repeat to complete the rows.

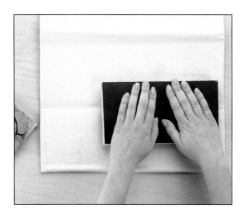

9 Remove the calico cover from the back of the chair and lay it out flat. Using tailor's chalk, mark the positions for the motifs along a line 5cm/2in in from each side. Load the stem stamp with green fabric paint and position the bottom edge on the marked line.

10 Load the rose stamp with pink fabric paint to complete the stamped design. Leave to dry, then rub off the chalk marks and fix the fabric paints according to the manufacturer's instructions.

PLASTER WALL TREATMENT

Add an extra dimension to stamping by creating a relief effect on your walls. For this technique, a mixture of paint and interior filler (Spackle) is applied to the stamp and then pressed on to the wall, leaving a raised motif. A monochromatic scheme suits this look best.

You will need

- matt emulsion (flat latex) paint in off-white, lime white and stone white
- wallpaper paste
- paint-mixing container
- large and medium decorator's paintbrushes
- 45cm/18in square of card (stock)
- pencil
- high-density sponge, such as upholstery foam
- felt-tipped pen or white crayon
- craft knife
- interior filler (Spackle)

1 Mix the off-white emulsion (latex) with 50 per cent wallpaper paste. Apply to the walls with a large paintbrush, working at random angles and keeping the effect quite rough.

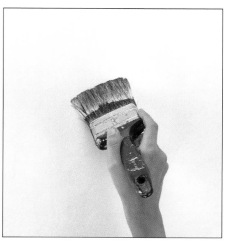

2 Apply random patches of lime white emulsion, allowing the off-white base coat to show in areas.

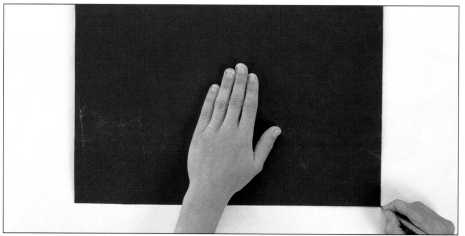

3 Using the card (stock) square as a template and beginning in a corner of the room, make a small mark at each corner of the card. Reposition the card using the previous marks as a guide and repeat to form a grid of evenly spaced marks around the room.

4 Copy the template at the back of the book and transfer it to a piece of high-density sponge. Cut away the excess sponge using a craft knife.

5 Using a medium paintbrush, mix stone white emulsion with interior filler (Spackle), using about 1 part filler to 3 parts paint.

6 Apply the mixture thickly to the stamp using a dabbing motion.

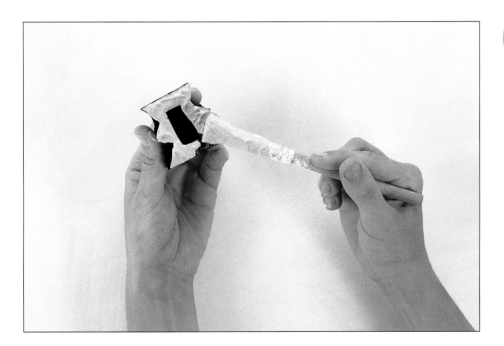

7 Print over each pencil mark,
pressing the stamp quite hard and
pulling it cleanly away – be careful not
to smear the impression. Leave for about
4 hours to dry.

8 Dry brush a little lime white
emulsion over each stamp, so that
only the areas in highest relief pick up
the paint. Do not attempt to make all
the motifs the same – the charm of this
technique lies in the slight irregularities.

GOTHIC DINING ROOM

Create a dramatic setting for candlelit dinner parties with purple and gold panels that will shimmer from deep velvety green walls. The effect is achieved by stamping the wall or walls with gold size and then rubbing on Dutch gold leaf which will adhere to the stamped motifs.

1 To make a template for the wall panels, draw a freehand arc from the centre top of the card (stock) square to the lower corner.

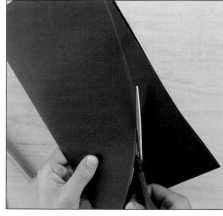

2 Fold the card in half down the centre and cut out both sides to make a symmetrical Gothic arch shape.

3 Copy the design from the back of the book and make a paper pattern with a diameter of 10cm/4in. Transfer the design on to a piece of high-density sponge. Cut away the excess sponge using a craft knife.

4 Apply dark green emulsion (latex) paint liberally to the wall or walls, using a sponge and working in a circular motion. Allow to dry.

5 Using a plumbline as a guide and beginning 23cm/9in from a corner, mark a vertical line up the wall to a height of 1.8m/6ft.

6 Measure across the wall and use the plumbline to draw vertical lines every 60cm/2ft.

7 Measure out 15cm/6in each side of each vertical and draw two more lines to mark the edges of the panels.

8 Place the point of the card template at the centre top point of each panel and draw in the curves.

9 Use a small paint roller to load the stamp with gold size. Print each panel, beginning with the centre top and working down the central line, then down each side.

10 When the size is tacky, apply Dutch gold leaf by rubbing over the backing paper with a soft brush.

11 Once the panel is complete, use the soft brush to remove any excess gold leaf.

12 Using only the centre of the stamp, fill in the spaces between the gold motifs using purple emulsion paint.

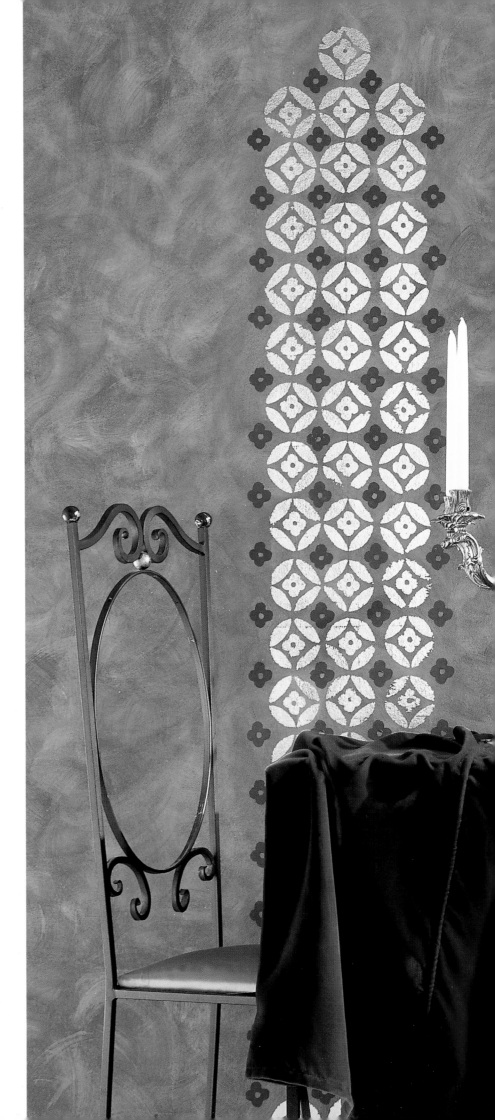

SCANDINAVIAN BEDROOM

This delicate stamped decoration on walls and woodwork is designed to go with the pale colours and painted furniture that characterize period Scandinavian interiors. This is a scheme of great charm, restful on the eye and perfect for a bedroom.

1 Mix grey-blue emulsion (latex) with 50 per cent wallpaper paste and apply to the walls with a broad paintbrush, working at random angles. Blend the brushstrokes to avoid hard edges.

2 Allow to dry, then repeat the process to soften the effect.

3 Mix off-white emulsion with 75 per cent wallpaper paste. Brush on as before. Allow to dry.

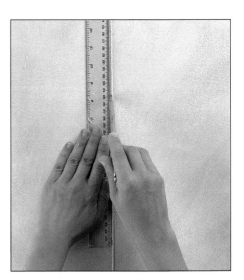

4 Hang a plumbline 2.5cm/1in from one corner and use as a guide to draw a vertical line down the wall.

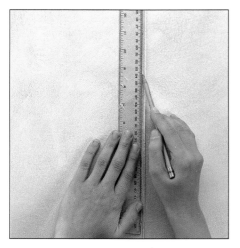

5 Measure about 40cm/16in across and draw a second vertical line, again using the plumbline as a guide. Repeat all around the room.

6 Trace the template at the back of the book and draw it on a rectangle of high-density sponge using a felt-tipped pen or white crayon. Cut away the excess sponge around the design using a craft knife.

7 Use a small paint roller to load the stamp with off-white emulsion (latex) paint.

8 Add details in red and grey-blue, using a fine artist's paintbrush over the off-white paint.

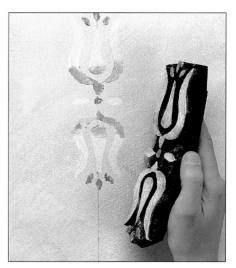

9 Apply the stamp to the wall, positioning it centrally over the marked line.

10 Repeat, positioning the stamp so that each motif is just touching the preceding one. Work down from the top of the wall.

11 Use the grey-blue wash mixed for the wall base coat to drag the door. Applying pressure to the bristles, pull down in a straight line, following the direction of the wood grain.

12 Apply the paint to the stamp as before, but this time loading only one flower motif. Stamp a single motif diagonally into the corners of each door panel as shown.

13 Add more paint to the grey-blue wash to deepen the colour. Edge the door panels using the artist's paintbrush. Leave to dry, then apply two coats of varnish to the door to protect the design.

ANIMAL FRIEZE

A low frieze is perfect for a nursery as it concentrates interest at the child's own level. Children can't fail to be enchanted by this harmonious troop of animals all sharing the same flowery field, with clouds billowing overhead.

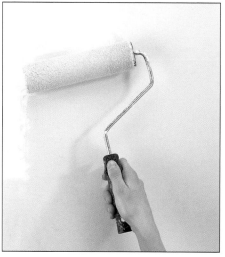

1 Paint the wall in sky blue emulsion (latex) using a paint roller. Leave to dry.

2 Paint the skirting (base) board in grass green emulsion.

3 Using the same green paint, apply wispy strokes up the wall to create the effect of grass growing up the wall. Allow the paint to dry.

4 Using a fine artist's paintbrush, highlight the grass with a lighter, yellowy green.

5 Paint small daisies in white emulsion at random in the grass. Add yellow centres.

6 Using a black inkpad and rubber stamp, stamp the cow motif randomly along the top of the frieze.

7 Print groups of chickens, using a brown inkpad.

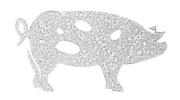

8 Print the pig stamp several times facing the opposite direction, using a pink inkpad.

9 Print the sheep, using black ink. Using the fine paintbrush, fill in the body of the sheep in white emulsion. Do the same with the cows if you wish.

10 Lightly press a natural sponge into white emulsion and sponge cloud shapes on the sky blue wall above the frieze.

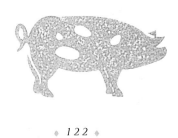

TEMPLATES

The templates on the following pages may be re-sized to any scale required. The simplest way of doing this is to enlarge or reduce them on a photocopier. Alternatively, trace the design and draw a grid of evenly spaced squares over your tracing. Draw a larger grid on another piece of paper and copy the outline square by square. Draw over the lines to make sure they are continuous.

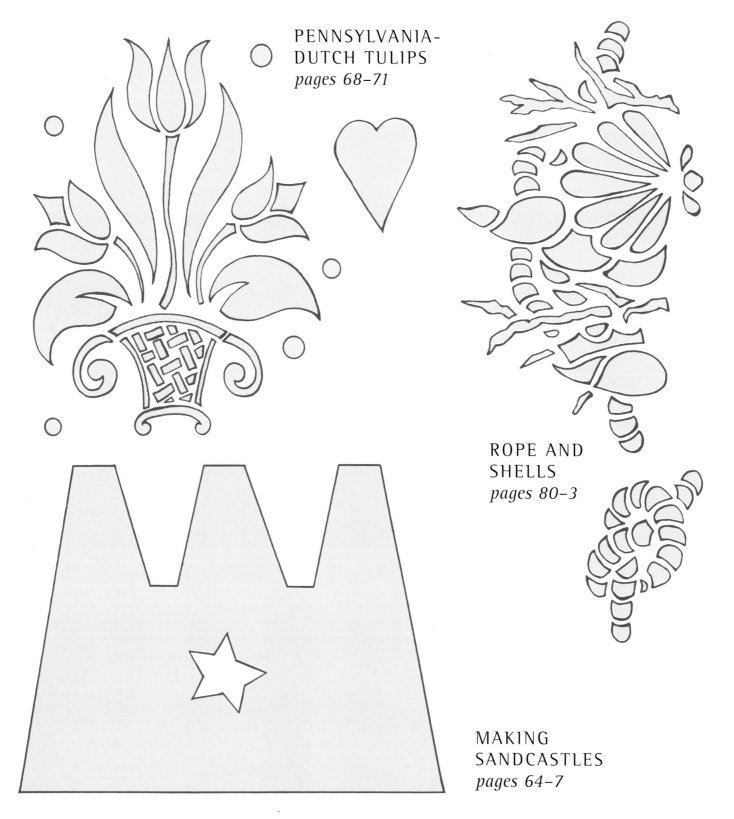

PENNSYLVANIA-DUTCH TULIPS
pages 68–71

ROPE AND SHELLS
pages 80–3

MAKING SANDCASTLES
pages 64–7

THROUGH
THE
GRAPEVINE
pages 76–9

HERALDIC
DINING ROOM
pages 84–7

Cut out the darker
areas for the
highlight templates

RENAISSANCE
ART
pages 72–5

CELESTIAL CHERUBS
pages 88–91

MOORISH TILE EFFECT
pages 96–9

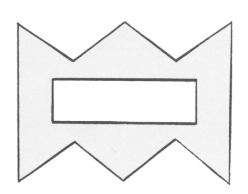

PLASTER WALL TREATMENT
pages 108–11

SANTA FE LIVING ROOM
pages 100–3

GOTHIC DINING ROOM
pages 112–15

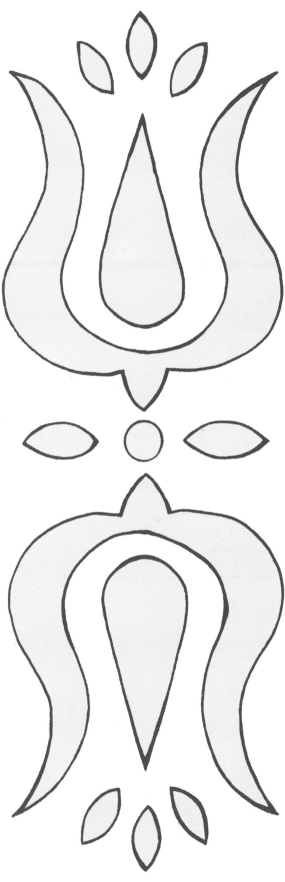

ART NOUVEAU ROSES
pages 104–7

SCANDINAVIAN BEDROOM
pages 116–19

INDEX